WASN'T IT
SMART
OF GOD TO...

CHAPMAN

HARVEST HOUSE PUBLISHERS

EUGENE, OREGON

WASN'T IT SMART OF GOD TO...
Copyright © 2012 by Steve Chapman
Published by Harvest House Publishers
Eugene, Oregon 97402
www.harvesthousepublishers.com

ISBN 978-0-7369-4654-4 (pbk.)
ISBN 978-0-7369-4655-1 (eBook)

Printed in the United States of America

12 13 14 15 16 17 18 19 20 / BP-SK / 10 9 8 7 6 5 4 3 2 1

A big thank-you to these contributors:

Annie Chapman

Heidi Beall

Nathan Chapman

Paul J. Chapman

Lillian Chapman

Dana Bacon

Bob Hughey

Jay Houston

Barbara Gordon

Peggy Dickerson

Fun Times

When our family of four was traveling together as itinerate musicians back in the late 1900s, we spent countless hours in vehicles covering the miles necessary to get to the next engagement. Those long rides were sometimes grueling and tough to endure, especially for our children. However, it was during one of those seemingly endless drives that the idea was conceived for the book you now hold in your hands.

It was around the summer of 1989. Our daughter, Heidi, was not far from becoming a "ten-ager" and our son, Nathan, was headed to his teens. We were on another long highway in a Midwestern plains state, and the car was quiet except for the constant sound of the rolling tires and air conditioner fan. Our two young "road warriors" were quietly staring out their windows with expressions that revealed the pain of boredom...again.

I looked at our kids through the rearview mirror and then nodded to Annie to take a look. She turned around for a glance, and when she turned back our eyes met. Without saying a word, we both knew we felt totally guilty that we were dragging them through the tediousness of so much traveling.

I turned my eyes back to the road and probably went on to think about the songs we'd be singing that night and my checklist of preconcert duties. My wife, Annie, however, did not put aside her motherly compassion. Embracing the emotions of the moment, she decided to attempt to lift our kids out of the highway doldrums. She broke the silence.

"Hey kids, let's play a game!" Annie announced.

The kids looked with reserved interest at their mom.

Annie continued: "Let's take turns finishing this sentence, 'Wasn't it smart of God to…' and you can include your thoughts about how practical His creation is—whether it's about our bodies, or nature, or whatever comes to your mind. I'll go first."

My ears perked up at that point, and I wondered what was in the mind of my brilliant wife. What I heard next was ingenious—so much so that it started our family down one of the most enjoyable conversation trails we can remember.

"Wasn't it smart of God to…," Annie paused for effect before finishing, "to make our nose holes go down instead of up so when it rains we don't drown."

I looked at Annie and smiled as we heard the kids

laugh. They immediately started audibly brainstorming additions to the list.

Heidi spoke up. "Wasn't it smart of God to…make our hair not bleed when we cut it."

We all smiled and agreed.

Nathan grinned as he added, "Wasn't it smart of God to…give us lips so when we kiss our teeth don't bang together." (Leave it to a near-teenage boy to come up with that one!)

It was my turn. "Wasn't it smart of God to…give us armpits *and* gravity to keep our arms down."

We were quickly on a roll, and there was lots of applause offered for each contribution to the game. Needless to say, the rest of the miles on that trip remain some of our most memorable. Thankfully, Annie grabbed a pen and paper and logged the quips we came up with that day. She added to the list as, from time to time during the rest of our tour, we continued our musings on "Wasn't it smart of God to…"

When we got home, that paper was filed away in our "favorite memory" file. It stayed there for more than twenty years—until I saw it again while going through some old boxes. I felt a rush of enjoyment as I perused the list and remembered the good time we'd had. I thought, *Perhaps it's time to let the rest of the world enjoy the fun our family had during that weekend of traveling*.

So drawing from that list and adding more, along

with additions from our now-grown children, their spouses, our extended family, and good friends, this little book was written to let you taste the sweet fruit of family fun. And just maybe these quirky and provocative thoughts will inspire you to start this tradition with your family and friends.

Whenever you read this book, whether solo on a beach, during a long highway journey, or with friends around a dinner table, my sincere hope is twofold. May it provide some interesting insights into the practicality of our marvelous Creator and may it spark your own creative endings for the truth, "Wasn't it smart of God to…"

Steve Chapman

Wasn't it smart of God to...

... make our nose holes go down instead of up so when it rains we won't drown.

... put our feet as far as possible from our noses.

... make aging a slow process instead of a sudden change, like while at youth camp.

Wasn't it smart of God to...

••• make us sleep with our eyes closed so we won't see our spouses sleeping with their mouths open.

••• give a new dad nine months to prepare for how much his life will drastically change.

••• make us so that during our teen years we have lots of little pimples instead of one huge one.

Wasn't it smart of God to...

... make our knees knobby so when we kneel to pray we will feel just enough discomfort to keep us alert and focused.

... give us hard knuckles so we can knock on doors.

... give us hormones so we'll want to mate... and have offspring who will want to mate...so we can have grandchildren.

Wasn't it smart of God to...

... give us fevers so we'll know when we're sick or in love.

... give us lips so when we kiss we don't bang our teeth together.

... give us 32 teeth so if we lose a few we still have some to chew with.

Wasn't it smart of God to...

... make a baby's voice high and shrill so the sound will wake dads from a deep sleep so they can wake up the moms.

... make our backsides padded so sitting will be more comfortable.

... design our legs to bend forward so when we kneel on the floor we don't mash our toes.

Wasn't it smart of God to...

••• pack all our vital organs into our torsos so if we lose an arm or leg we'll still be alive.

••• let hearing loss generally happen in our later years so we don't have to listen to our aging friends complain about joint pain, bowel issues, memory loss, and...*I said, "Joint pain, bowel issues, memory loss..."*

••• give us ears and noses to hold up our glasses.

... give labor in childbirth to clue in mothers about what the rest of their lives will be like.

... make the balding process slow instead of all of a sudden, like while on a date.

... make the diameter of the index finger slightly smaller than the diameter of nose holes.

Wasn't it smart of God to...

••• give us shoulders to hold up our shirts.

••• make our heads not turn all the way around—probably because it would just be too creepy.

••• make us so we sneeze out instead of in.

■■■ give us two eyebrows instead of one—and tweezers to help keep them that way.

■■■ not make the hair in our ears grow as long as the hair on our heads. (And give us friends who are kind enough to tell us if we're the exception.)

... give us a keen sense of hearing so we'll know when dinner is ready.

... give us sight so we can look back to see what we tripped over 'cause we weren't watching where we were going.

... give us the alphabet so we can quickly go through it when we can't remember some-one's name at a reunion.

Wasn't it smart of God to...

... give us old age to help us look forward to heaven.

... put our noses close to our mouths so smelling food before we eat it is more convenient.

... give us tongues so when we talk we don't "hown ike ikh."

... give us a sense of touch so we'll know the joy of feeling a baby's soft skin.

... make our lower jaws move when we talk instead of our upper jaws so when we talk our heads don't violently bounce up and down.

... make our arms not as long as our legs so they don't drag on the ground when we walk.

Wasn't it smart of God to...

... make our ears protrude for catching sound waves.

... give us enough hair to fill the gap between the outer edges of our ears and our heads...or to cover our ears if we want to.

... make our noses flare when more air is needed during vigorous exercise or arguing.

Wasn't it smart of God to...

... give us two eyes instead of just one so we can still see to drive with one while rubbing the other.

... make our feet long and flat on the bottom instead of pointy stubs so the poem "Footprints in the Sand" wouldn't be "Little Round Pointy Holes in the Sand."

... give us hips to hold up our pants.

... give us fingernails so that blackboards can have a dual purpose.

... make us so smiling takes more effort than frowning to remind us to work at being kind.

... give us armpits *and* gravity to keep our arms down.

Wasn't it smart of God to...

... give us receding hairlines instead of advancing ones.

... make our eyes blink so we can moisten them as well as understand how quickly life goes by.

... make our fingernails grow four times faster than our toenails.

... make our arms foldable for staying warm
and for showing coolness during a spat.

... give us ear wax instead of ear honey.

... make our stomachs with folds that
expand as they fill up so we don't explode
if we cave and eat that third piece of cake.

Wasn't it smart of God to...

... give us nose hair to help filter the air we breathe to help keep our lungs clean.

... give us inquisitive minds so we can ask questions that He will answer so we'll know more about Him.

... cause women to forget the extent of pain during childbirth so we can know the joy of siblings.

Wasn't it smart of God to...

... design humans to yawn so we'll know we're sleepy or that our dates are bored.

... give us two ears and one mouth so we'll remember to listen twice as much as we talk.

... make our hair not bleed when we cut it.

Wasn't it smart of God to...

... give us free environmental cleanup crews consisting of buzzards and other carrion eaters so we don't have to deal with dead critters that are rotten and smelly.

... design us in such a way that the 50,000 cells that die in our bodies while we're reading this book won't rot and smell bad, thus eliminating the embarrassing buzzards-over-our-heads potential.

... make giraffes able to clean their own ears with their 21-inch tongues so we don't have to do it for them with our stubby ones.

... make our left lungs smaller than our right lungs to make room for our hearts.

... create the woodpecker with the amazing ability to peck 20 times per second and not get a headache.

Wasn't it smart of God to...

... give us a sense of smell so we'll know when it's time for a bath—or a friend's bath.

... make our bodies using enough phosphorus to cover 2200 match heads but not ignite while we're filing our nails.

... make us able to wink so we can communicate important information without words.

Wasn't it smart of God to...

... create the human body using enough carbon to make 900 pencils—yet not leave dark gray marks on our bedsheets.

... make the human body with enough fat to make seven bars of soap—yet not turn into mounds of suds when we're caught in the rain.

... design the adult human body able to hold enough water to fill a 10-gallon tank *and* give us bladders to hold any excess (at least temporarily).

Wasn't it smart of God to...

... make ants so they don't sleep. (That's our only revenge!)

... lead us to discover the wheel. (Otherwise there would be a lot of cars on blocks.)

... give us fire to use for warmth, energy, manufacturing, and marshmallows.

Wasn't it smart of God to...

... make rain fall in lots of little drops instead of one really big one.

... make babies so adorable that we don't really mind cleaning up the unbelievable messes they can make.

... make the healthiest foods the most colorful and delightful to our eyes.

Wasn't it smart of God to...

... make human bone as strong as granite and able to support up to nine tons—a feature especially valuable after Thanksgiving dinner.

... make the human blood cell able to make a complete circuit of the body in about 60 seconds—guaranteeing that at least part of us is getting exercise.

Wasn't it smart of God to...

••• make the muscles of our eyes able to move approximately 100,000 times a day without breaking a sweat.

••• cover our entire body with skin that flakes and sheds at a rate of up to 105 pounds during 70 years of living—and thankfully not all at once.

••• give us nails to bite when we're nervous that aren't made of metal and don't taste like Brussels sprouts.

Wasn't it smart of God to...

... design us so our feet are so far from our teeth that we can't comfortably chew our toenails when we're grown-ups. (This restriction prevents joint injuries and salvages personal dignity.)

... give us 300,000 or so little blood vessels in our lungs that would stretch 1500 miles if laid end to end—but thankfully aren't.

Wasn't it smart of God to...

... make our stomach digestive acids strong enough to dissolve zinc. (This feature is especially important if we happen to swallow a flashlight battery.)

... put our noses close to our mouths so we can discreetly and quickly check our breath before our dates open the door.

Wasn't it smart of God to...

... not put eyes in the back of our heads. (I'm sure my third-grade teacher had them though.)

... say to the serpent that deceived Eve in the Garden of Eden, "Cursed are you...You will crawl on your belly and you will eat dust all the days of your life," so Satan wouldn't have a leg to stand on.

Wasn't it smart of God to...

... enclose the sea so we don't have to swim all the time.

"Who shut up the sea behind doors...
I fixed limits for it and set its doors and bars
in place, when I said, 'This far you may come
and no farther; here is where your proud
waves halt'?" (Job 38:8,10-11).

Wasn't it smart of God to...

... design the sneeze to "share" up to 40,000 droplets of contaminated moisture in a spray that can exceed 200 miles per hour. (You've been warned!)

... give sneezers and unfortunate bystanders the gift of soft Kleenex.

... make us incapable of sneezing with our eyes open, sparing us from seeing the stranger next to us roll his eyes in disgust while wiping his face because we didn't grab a Kleenex in time.

Wasn't it smart of God to...

... give some people curly hair and others straight hair so we would learn how to conquer our tendency to envy.

... put flowers deep in the forest, colorful fish in the depths of the oceans, and huge nebulas high in the heavens to give us something to discover.

Wasn't it smart of God to...

... put iron, copper, and other ores in the ground and give us the ingenuity to dig them up, process them, and make tools.

... give us a sense of taste so chocolate isn't a wasted resource.

Wasn't it smart of God to...

... make a single strand of DNA into an information storage unit that is a thousand times thinner than a strand of hair yet capable of holding enough information to fill a stack of books that would stretch from the earth to the moon 500 times.

... design us so that even if we are twins our fingerprints are different, assuring us that we are unique individuals.

Wasn't it smart of God to...

... make us with two thumbs for gripping
and to stick up to show double approval
to our kids for jobs well done!

... make rainbows appear after it rains to
remind us that He's keeping His promise
to not send a global-wide flood.

... place our hearts behind a protective cage of
hard ribs and the sternum. (This wonderful design is great when batters smoke line
drives at the mound and we're pitching!)

Wasn't it smart of God to...

... give us graphite that contains carbon—
a key component of diamonds and lead.
(Instead of buying an expensive diamond
for his sweetheart, a fellow could just give
her a pencil!)

... put 8000 taste buds on the human
tongue's upper surface—a number that
matches the choices of food at many
church potlucks.

Wasn't it smart of God to...

... make each taste bud cell renew every seven to ten days. (So go ahead, thaw those leftovers from last week!)

... make our digestive tract 29.5 feet in length, which means we really can have our cake... and our friend's cake...and eat it too.

... make our sex cells contain only half the genetic material required to make another human being—a fact that gives extra meaning to His comment, "And the two shall become one."

Wasn't it smart of God to...

... make our tongues the strongest muscle in our bodies, proportionally speaking, so we can lift the spirits of our families and friends.

... give us many salivary glands in our mouths that can produce a quart of saliva each day. (Another reason to avoid the front pew— and a possible drenching—when the preacher delivers a rousing sermon!)

Wasn't it smart of God to...

... include enough discomfort in the ninth month of pregnancy that women are more than willing to go through childbirth.

... make tooth enamel the hardest thing in our bodies. (Some of us have skulls that run a close second.)

Wasn't it smart of God to...

... make sea urchins brainless but able to survive through simple nerve cords located in their mouth area. (That feature is also given to relatives of the sea urchin: sea cucumbers, starfish, and, oddly enough, some politicians.)

... make our sense of smell an important part of tasting food—but diminish that attribute when we have bad colds and have to take nasty-tasting medicine.

Wasn't it smart of God to...

... give us a sense of smell 1000 times less effective than a beagle's. (Otherwise we'd probably spend most of our time chasing rabbits!)

... give us the ability to create nearly 10,000 facial expressions. (Unfortunately that number is reduced by 9999 after a Botox injection.)

... provide millions of dust mites to live in our beds and gobble up skin flakes that fall off us. (Which makes some people wonder, *Why change the sheets?*)

Wasn't it smart of God to...

... put assassins known as *lymphocytes* in each of us to identify, find, and kill disease-causing cells.

... put gizzards in birds that have no teeth and give them a tolerance for swallowing grit of various sizes to grind up seeds so they don't starve.

Wasn't it smart of God to...

••• give owls extremely flexible necks that can rotate nearly 360 degrees to compensate for their tubular eyes that don't roll. (Knowing this fact may help squelch the heebie-jeebies the next time an owl turns its head all the way around to look at us!)

••• create a magnetic field in the iron core of the earth strong enough to charge particles in space yet weak enough that metal things, such as nails, frying pans, and airplanes, don't stick to the ground.

Wasn't it smart of God to...

... create a black cow that eats green grass and makes white milk as part of producing yellow butter so we can shake our heads in udder amazement.

... make tigers able to see six times better in the dark than we can but run only four times faster than us. (Wait—that's not a comforting thought!)

... make some deer have white tails they can flash to help other deer follow them, to discourage predators, and to let hunters know they've been outsmarted again.

... make most male birds using brighter colors than their female counterparts to make courtship rituals interesting and patrolling territory more effective. (The equivalent of this colorful characteristic in human males can be seen in football stadiums where men paint themselves with bright colors and gather in territorial formations. Sadly, this may limit hopes for courtship.)

... make most female birds muted in color for better concealment on the nest. (Unfortunately there is no human equivalent of this unique feature, so women in "nesting" settings often frighten men.)

... make the bottom of toddlers' feet tough enough for walking barefoot yet sensitive enough for tickling fun.

... put our noses on our faces instead of under our arms—for odorously obvious reasons.

... place the nearest star close enough to the earth that we could vacation there if we only drove 100 mph for 29 million years. (Just imagine that family trip!)

Wasn't it smart of God to...

... give some men the divine inspiration to write the most popular and life-changing book of all times—the Bible. (With more than 6 billion copies in print, hopefully thieves will walk off with this book and let it radically improve their existence now and forever.)

... make the "poison-arrow" frog's defense potent enough to provide plenty of protection. (The poison is strong enough to kill 2200 people—a fact that tells the 2199 people in line behind the first victim to run.)

Wasn't it smart of God to...

... make baby robins capable of eating 14 feet of earthworms every day. (This brings to mind the obvious question: Do earthworms really have feet?)

... make gold so it never rusts—even if buried in the ground for a thousand years or worn on a finger for a lifetime.

... make the sun more than 300,000 times larger than the earth, design it to burn fiercely at 27 million degrees Fahrenheit, and put it 93,000 miles away from ice cream.

Wasn't it smart of God to...

... make a flea able to jump 350 times its body length. (The human equivalent is 14 city blocks!)

... make some species of ribbon worms capable of eating themselves if they can't find food. (Be thankful God didn't design us that way or "finger foods" would have a totally new meaning.)

Wasn't it smart of God to...

... design the female praying mantis to rip the head off of the male during or after mating so we will be thankful the Creator didn't include that characteristic in our makeup.

... design female worker honeybees so they die after stinging us. (It serves them right!)

... make the butterfly able to taste with its feet but not make us do the same—especially for those of us who never toss our old tennis shoes.

Wasn't it smart of God to...

... make our brains with more than 100 billion nerve cells and our skin with 45 miles or so of nerves so we're totally accurate when we tell someone, "You've got a lot of nerve!"

... give squirrels the instinct to bury nuts and a limited capacity to remember where they hid them so there will be more trees in the woods.

Wasn't it smart of God to...

... design dogs to understand 35 to 40 commands—an impressive capacity unrivaled by most husbands.

... see to it that cats, though part of His handiwork, were never mentioned in the Bible.

... make alligators—and most teenage boys—able to gulp down an eight-pound chicken in five seconds.

... create the human brain with the power to store 100 billion bits of information and the ability to recall most of it. (Except, unfortunately, birthdays, anniversaries, and exam answers.)

... make 80 percent of flowering plants able to fertilize themselves for reproduction—but thankfully not give humans that ability.

Wasn't it smart of God to...

... make the human scalp contain 100,000 hairs on average. (I'm sure I used to have that many...)

... design us to blink, on average, 6 million times a year...triple that number during the year we date and marry.

... make our eyelids with many short eyelashes instead of one really long one.

Wasn't it smart of God to...

... create the human strong and efficient enough to walk, on average, the equivalent of five times around the equator in a normal lifetime. (Half that distance is probably accumulated during round-trip treks from the TV room to the refrigerator!)

... design the human heart with enough pumping pressure to squirt blood 30 feet (but not for long).

▪▪▪ design us to sing when we're happy and cry when we're sad, and at other times, to cry when we're happy and sing when we're sad.

▪▪▪ give us the capacity to breathe around 23,400 times in a 24-hour period without giving it a lot of thought.

Wasn't it smart of God to...

... make the sparrow a small and seemingly inconsequential creature, yet by revealing how much He cares for it providing a heartwarming picture of how much He loves us.

Are not two sparrows sold for a penny? Yet not one of them will fall to the ground outside your Father's care...So don't be afraid; you are worth more than many sparrows (Matthew 10:29,31).

Wasn't it smart of God to...

... make our bodies able to feel pain as a
warning that we're hurt and give us tears
so others know we're not kidding.

... give us snow, firewood, chimneys, hot
apple cider, and friends.

... create us with vocal cords that vibrate
when air is passed through them so we can
make intelligible sounds to communicate.
(Yes, men have this capability too!)

Wasn't it smart of God to...

... "wire" humans with an uncanny ability to communicate with body motions, such as shaking the head side to side to mean no, up and down to mean yes, and combined with a tilt of the head, lifting of shoulders and hands and eyebrows, to mean "Whatevah!"

... put muscles in our toes so we can wiggle them vigorously—especially while sitting for hours on a deer stand in the woods or at Lambeau Field in Green Bay, Wisconsin, in late December.

Wasn't it smart of God to...

... give us sweat glands on our foreheads that produce a different kind of moisture than our armpits so when we get nervous at least our faces won't stink.

... make us unable to tickle ourselves so we can wash the bottoms of our feet and under our arms without uncontrollable laughter.

Wasn't it smart of God to...

... give us the intelligence to mark time and the ingenuity to make devices that can assist in this ability so we won't be late for church.

... make nose hair not grow as long as the hair on our heads...and small scissors to keep it that way.

... rig life in such a way that none of us can do it well without His help.

[God] marked out their appointed times in history and the boundaries of their lands. God did this so that [we] would seek him and perhaps reach out for him and find him, though he is not far from any one of us. "For in him we live and move and have our being" (Acts 17:26-28).

Wasn't it smart of God to...

... make the palms of our hands flat so we can write notes to ourselves on them—and give us the ability to fold our hands when we don't want anyone to know what we wrote.

... make our bodies with built-in spare parts, such as toes, feet, legs, fingers, arms, shoulders, eyes, and ears—but wisely giving each of us only one mouth.

Wasn't it smart of God to...

... design women to produce milk only after childbirth and only long enough to feed the child until it's weaned.

... provide a woman with a womb that expands up to 500 times its size to accommodate a growing baby but returns to its original size after birthing—making it unnecessary to discard prepregnancy clothing.

... give us fingernails on both hands so we can clean under the fingernails on both hands.

... design us so we can fold up to half our size in height. (This handy feature is especially useful when our beds are short-sheeted at youth camp.)

... make women's senses heighten dramatically during pregnancy, allowing them to smell chocolate up to five miles in any direction.

... bless some men with competitive natures and athletic ability and give some people the ingenuity to invent games and build stadiums. That way the rest of us can enjoy watching our favorite sports teams play. (Go, Giants!)

... put trees on the earth that mankind can use to make paper on which he can make designs for buildings that he can build using the trees he didn't use for making paper.

... create in advance all the material necessary for people to build anything they want or need throughout time so nothing more is added to the universe that might make the earth heavier and cause it to fall out of its perfectly placed position in the universe.

... make all humans basically the same on the inside so surgeons don't have to guess where things are when making incisions.

Wasn't it smart of God to...

... build a natural thermostat into our bodies, along with the ability to form sweat, to help cool us down by ten degrees or so during heat waves.

... build a shivering reflex into our bodies to help warm us up by 10 degrees or so during extreme cold.

... build into our bodies the ability to generate a lukewarm clamminess to let nurses know when the other two attributes have stopped working.

Wasn't it smart of God to...

... give us 10 toes so if we stub one we still have 9 that don't hurt.

... help people invent Odor Eaters to put into our shoes since He also put 250,000 or so odor-producing sweat glands in each foot.

... put enough iron in a human body to make at least a one-inch nail. (I have yet to meet anyone who has found theirs.)

Wasn't it smart of God to...

... make the cells in our bodies so small that if we could look really, really close we'd see that it takes 200 or so of them to cover each of the periods and tittles (dots over the letter "i") used in this short paragraph. (How many cells would that be?)*

... make our ears continue to grow through-out our lifetimes so in our old age when our hearing worsens they're at their larg-est and, thus, at their maximum sound-capturing capacity. (Plus it's that time in life when we don't really give a hoot what people think about the size of our ears.)

---

* 14 dots x 200 = 2800 cells. Did you count the three dots in the ellipses and the dots in the question marks?

Wasn't it smart of God to...

••• provide husbands and wives examples
of true devotion through the behavior
of some animals. (Various birds, includ-
ing Canada geese and doves, mate for life.
Wolves are also loyal mates.)

••• put an iris in each human eye that shrinks
the pupil to protect the retina when the
eye is suddenly flooded with bright light,
such as the sun or that intensely brilliant
light used in interrogation rooms.

... design the human brain to triple in weight between birth and adulthood—but wrinkle as it grows so it will fit inside our skulls. (Speaking of brain wrinkles, if you removed your brain and flattened it with an iron it would cover an extra large ironing board—but that would really hurt!)

... put a half-moon shaped area at the bottom of our fingernails called the "lanula" so we'll always have something to look at and say, "I wonder why that's there."

Wasn't it smart of God to...

... give us two hands so we can lend one to a neighbor when he or she needs it.

... make the human body contain enough sulfur to kill all the fleas on an average-sized dog—providing a good argument for letting your bluetick coonhound sleep in your bed.

... give fishermen an abiding expectancy so they never tire of tossing a line.

Wasn't it smart of God to...

... make human saliva glands produce about 25,000 quarts of spit in an average lifetime—enough to fill two swimming pools. (Care to take a dip? You first!)

... give us the medical insight to assign types to blood, such as the common "O" type, which also has variations: "O+," "O-," and "O no!"

... make 300 million cells die in the human body every minute. (Many preachers wish God would do the same for cell phones during sermons!)

Wasn't it smart of God to...

••• design women's hearts to beat faster than men's—especially when a man is on one knee in front of the woman he loves.

••• put five to six quarts of blood in the average healthy human. (That's a similar quantity to oil put in a V8 engine! But engine oil has to be replaced every 3000 miles or six months while blood is self-replicating. So why not put blood in engines?)

Wasn't it smart of God to...

... make every human with a unique tongue print that can be easily lifted if a criminal happens to open the door with his or her tongue.

... design the African cicada fly to spend 17 years sleeping, wake up for two weeks to mate, and then die. (Pity those who over-sleep!)

... design each human body with the capacity to consume 50 tons of food and drink 13,000 gallons of liquid—but not in one sitting.

... make the human jaw muscle strong enough to create up to 200 pounds of chewing force—a capacity especially useful when eating your spouse's first pot roast.

... give porcupines about 30,000 quills and make them loose enough that if threatened they can "let go" of their quills to protect themselves and make predators consider them a poor source of food.

... design camel humps to absorb heat
and keep it from getting to the internal
organs—and to also frighten tourists who
climb on for the first time.

... create cats and humans with very different
ideas when it comes to personal hygiene.

... put eyebrows above our eye sockets to
help keep the sweat out of our eyes and
give parents a means of warning their kids
of impending unhappiness.

... design us so our eyesight dims in our older years, which smooths out the wrinkles when we look in the mirror.

... give us all a painless and free way to determine which eye is dominant. (Make a circle with your right-hand fingers, hold it at arm's length from your face, look through the circle with both eyes and find an object. Now slowly bring your hand toward your face, keeping the object in the circle. The eye that maintains the object in the circle is your dominant one.)

... give us a propensity for being either right- or left-handed, with most of the people favoring their right hands. (This is a wonderful thing since the majority of baseball gloves are made for right-handed players.)

... design a few of us to be ambidextrous—a rare ability found mostly in ravenous, growing boys anywhere free hotdogs are found!

... make the skin in the bendable areas of our bodies a bit tougher and baggier to accommodate the space the joints need.

... design rats with an inability to vomit, which motivates them to nibble first to determine if the food will make them sick before fully consuming it. (This technique might be wise for humans who enjoy unique dining experiences.)

Wasn't it smart of God to...

... create a plant that shakes its leaves even
when there is no wind. (The Telegraph
Plant grows in Asia and the South Pacific.)
This unique trait can also be seen in the
knees of novice singers just before and
during first-time performances!

... give the Bombardier Beetle the ability to
defend itself by shooting boiling liquid
out of its abdomen. (Thankfully, this is an
ability He withheld from people.)

Wasn't it smart of God to...

... provide the hummingbird with an amazing talent for flying since its legs and feet are not designed for walking.

... give "cleaner fish" an appetite for old, rotten food particles found in the mouths of sharks and other large fish—and the courage to swim inside and eat up.

Wasn't it smart of God to...

... make two-thirds of the earth's surface ocean. (And where there are oceans there are sunny beaches!)

... allow us the ability to develop technology that measures heat. (The hottest day in modern history was 136 degrees Fahrenheit in El Azizia, Libya—a fact menopausal women can use to accurately describe hot flashes!)

... make the distance to the center of the earth an amazing 3963 miles and provide an outer skin that is 41 miles thick. (Proportionally, that's the ratio of the peel to the fruit in an average apple.)

... make the mosquito so it doesn't actually bite. (Unfortunately, the female mosquito stabs and then sucks our blood because she needs it to lay eggs.)

Wasn't it smart of God to...

... design male mosquitoes so they don't need our blood, thereby decreasing our danger of getting stabbed by mosquitoes. (Male mosquitoes dine on plant nectar.)

... design rabbits so they can see completely behind themselves. (If humans could do that, the mirror business would decline.)

... create a world that contains more chickens than humans—and then make us big enough so we won't get eaten by them.

Wasn't it smart of God to...

... design female lions with a willingness to hunt more than male lions. (Males prefer to rest, which gives new meaning to "He's just lion around"!)

... provide humans with the gift of fire. (Otherwise, according to some scientists, we'd have to yell for eight years, seven months, and six days to produce enough sonic energy to heat one cup of coffee.)

... make it impossible for us to lick our elbows. (If there ever comes a time when you can lick your elbow, you might want to call 911.)

... design the human mind to contain and use, on average, a vocabulary of 6000 words. (This capacity was expanded by our kids while on family vacations.)

Wasn't it smart of God to...

... make bee honey, a food that does not spoil, suitable for man and animal. (Enjoying delicious honey—what a wonderful way to honor such tedious and hard teamwork!)

... make mighty oak trees grow from tiny acorns to remind us that great things in life often have small beginnings.

Wasn't it smart of God to...

... use the simple word "if" to help us understand the awesome truth that we have the privilege of working *with* Him to bring about His promises for our lives.

If we confess our sins, he is faithful and just and will forgive us our sins and purify us from all unrighteousness (1 John 1:9).

Wasn't it smart of God to...

... not play "hide and seek" with us. (Instead He plays "seek and find" and promises our success!)

"You will seek me and find me when you seek me with all your heart. I will be found by you," declares the LORD (Jeremiah 29:13-14).

... allow us to experience only the fringe of His greatness and a whisper of His awe-someness because He knows we wouldn't understand His thunderous power.

Wasn't it smart of God to...

... give each of us a dominant foot and leg. (This surprisingly significant trait especially impacts the kicking motion. Kicking with the nondominant side looks comical, so why not make it a rule that football kickers have to use their nondominant side. That would certainly up the entertainment value!)

... delay the gland secretions in the hooves of whitetail fawns so the newborns can't be trailed by coyotes and other predators with a keen sense of smell.

Wasn't it smart of God to...

... make the bison "head to toe" usable by Native Americans. (From tender meat to the strong sinew used for bindings and thread, from the hide used for clothing to the bile as an ingredient in yellow paint, the bison was truly a "department store on the hoof.")

... put hair on our heads to protect our scalps from the blistering effects of the hot sun in summer and provide warmth in the cold seasons. (Unfortunately, some of us have to resort to ball caps.)

... give humans a sense of humor that generates laughter, which in turn contributes to better health, which in turn gives us more to smile about.

A joyful heart is good medicine
(Proverbs 17:22 NASB).

... put a bony little bump on the outside area of our wrists so our watches won't slide down too far.

Wasn't it smart of God to...

••• let us discover that a string tightly stretched between two anchor points over wood can make beautiful music when plucked...or send an arrow on a straight flight. (Music and archery—both are just fine with me!)

••• put seeds in an apple that can be counted, but put so many apples in those seeds that it's impossible to number them.

••• give us the gift of bat guano (dung) that
makes excellent fertilizer because of its
rich nutrients. (Since the Civil War, bat
guano has been used to produce gunpow-
der and other explosives because of its
high nitrogen content.)

••• design us with the very important feature
called memory. (This is especially useful
in helping us avoid making the same mis-
take twice!)

Wasn't it smart of God to...

... make nighttime arrive gradually instead of suddenly, especially when we're in the middle of an unfamiliar bend in the highway on a hot motorcycle!

... make daytime arrive gradually so we have time to escape after TP-ing a friend's yard.

Wasn't it smart of God to...

... give wings to birds so they can fly, to give some people the brains to figure out how people can fly, and to provide enough sky for both species to enjoy the experience.

... let us know that His "power is made perfect in weakness" since weakness is one thing we have plenty of.

Wasn't it smart of God to...

... make the human body with some of the same base and trace elements found in soil. This way when we're returned to the earth as dust, we're not pollutants (Genesis 3:19).

[Jesus said], "Whoever wants to become great among you must be your servant"... and "those who humble themselves will be exalted" (Matthew 20:26; 23:12).

Wasn't it smart of God to...

... design human hands so the fingers of a male interlock perfectly with the fingers of a female, creating an electrifying connection that can last a lifetime.

... give parents who want to continue to be great moms and dads to their adult children the example of a river to follow. (When a river stays in its banks it's a friend to those who live by it, but when it flows out of its banks it can do major damage.)

Wasn't it smart of God to...

... give raccoons fingers so nimble they can remove a dime from a shirt pocket, remove several dimes from a pants pocket, and hold them individually between their fingers. (This is a good reason to name a pet raccoon Zacchaeus, after the tax collector Jesus spent time with.)

... make the land area on the earth span 52,500,000 square miles—plenty of room to "turn that rig around."

... add waterfalls to the earth's surface, such as the massive Khone waterfall in Asia and Niagara Falls on the border of the United States and Canada, so that we can stand near them and hear the mighty roar and feel the awesome thunder. (Hopefully we can resist the strange urge to jump in for a swim.)

... give marine biologists the ability to discover that goldfish have a memory span of three seconds. (This information helps me feel better when I see a little goldfish leaving a pet store or carnival in a tiny plastic bag filled with water.)

Wasn't it smart of God to...

... make toucans' bills more than half as long
as their bodies. (This begs the question,
Why not take away their credit cards?)

... design road runners to run 15 miles an
hour and eat rattlesnakes whole. (This feat
is topped only by commuters who eat a
portion of a cow while traveling 75 miles
per hour.)

Wasn't it smart of God to...

... make the cute and humble sea otter a "keystone species" by giving it the environmentally important job of tending gardens of kelp in the seas and oceans. (With an appetite for kelp as well as the kelp-damaging urchins that destroy the plants, the sea otter's work is paramount to carefully managing the plants that many species depend on.)

... give humans the propensity to faint when facing perceived danger or overwhelming joy. (That unusual trait makes wedding ceremonies more interesting.)

Wasn't it smart of God to...

... create us with the ability to communicate through a written system that transcends the boundaries of place and time. (This allows previous generations to share their wisdom with future generations. If you're looking for a good reason to keep a journal, now you have it!)

... design boy babies to not grow beards. (It's hard enough to potty train them, much less teach them to use a razor. And the image of toddlers with full beards would be way too weird!)

Wasn't it smart of God to...

••• design us so we start out with 350 bones
and then reduce that number to 206
as we grow. (Thankfully He did this by
causing some bones to fuse together as
opposed to having bones pop through our
skin during vigorous activities.)

••• come to earth as a human baby so we
wouldn't be afraid or die from His awesome and indescribable presence.

Wasn't it smart of God to...

... give us wheat for making bread, tomatoes for making sauce, milk for making cheese, hogs for making sausage, soil for growing mushrooms, and iron for making ovens where all these things can be turned into hot pizza.

... design human legs perfect for straddling a horse or a Harley. (Both are safe to ride if handled with respect. Leather goes well with both. And neither one needs a wind-shield.)

... design Esau to be a skillful hunter and Jacob to be a quiet man living in tents so we know it's okay to be country folk or city slickers.

The boys grew up, and Esau became
a skillful hunter, a man of the open country,
while Jacob was a content to stay at home
among the tents (Genesis 25:27).

Wasn't it smart of God to...

... put within us the ingenuity to harness natural sources of power found in wind, fire, water, fossil fuels, sunlight, and bright smiles.

... give eyes to the eagle that can see straight ahead *and* to the side at the same time. (This astounding ability is matched only by mothers during church services.)

••• give the eagle the ability to see prey in
a three-square-mile area while flying at
1000 feet. (Almost as amazing is the technology that lets us look at our houses via
satellite using the internet!)

••• make the leaves fall from the trees in the
autumn to add a protective cover over
the ground for the cold months of winter.
(This fact of nature doesn't help us get out
of raking the yard though.)

Wasn't it smart of God to...

... give people the time and inclination to create effort-saving devices, such as sailing ships, plows, printing presses, internal combustion engines, telephones, chainsaws, and perhaps the most ingenious invention—the TV remote.

... send us into this world with nothing and then take us back with nothing so we're reminded that the most valuable thing in life is that we belong to Him.

Wasn't it smart of God to...

... say to the wealthy in this world, "Be rich in good deeds, and…be generous and willing to share," so they would know that prosperity isn't defined by money alone.

... make children washable and guaranteed not to shrink.

... give newborn children an innate need for their mothers' touch and mothers the irresistible urge to cuddle and hold them.

Wasn't it smart of God to...

... give children a mysteriously strong desire to hear their fathers say, "I love you" and give fathers the courage to say it.

... design the palm of our hands to sweat when we're nervous so we'll know whether or not the salesperson is trustworthy when we shake hands to close a deal.

... make the human body with the capacity to feel pain at the place it is injured. (Otherwise an actor who actually does "break a leg" during a performance wouldn't know to leave the stage immediately and get medical attention.)

... give us music to go with our memories—especially with pictures at wedding rehearsal dinners.

Wasn't it smart of God to...

... design our skin to expand due to extensive holiday excesses and to contract with New Year's resolution success.

... make the wind an unseen force and give us tree leaves, fields of wheat, tumbleweeds, and ocean waves as evidence that it exists. (That's like the Holy Spirit, except evidence of His existence is how He moves in our lives.)

Wasn't it smart of God to...

... let Adam give names to the animals. (It would be confusing if all creatures were called "What's that"!)

... design trees and dogs to have bark. (Coincidence? I don't think so!)

Wasn't it smart of God to...

••• put "strong stomachs" in select individuals so they can withstand the sight of blood and guts and become surgeons and medical personnel.

••• give us the courage to let those medical people work on us when we need it.

••• give us the intelligence to create an exchange system using metal coins and printed paper that can be traded for goods and services. (Without it, the guy at the door wouldn't leave the pizza we ordered!)

... create a grand-scale water conservation system using trees, grasses, and other foliage to help soak up and use rainwater and prevent oversaturation of the ground. (I tried using this information to get out of mowing the yard and trimming the hedges. It didn't work, so don't bother trying.)

... spare planet Earth's inhabitants from feeling the effects of the planet traveling through space at 67,000 miles per hour.

Wasn't it smart of God to...

... make a lightning bolt carry 100 million to 1 billion volts, producing a jolt that should make us glad the static electricity shock that happens when we shake hands after walking on carpet is only 20,000 to 25,000 volts. (For comparison, in the United States, household electrical current is around 100 volts.)

... give the alligator 2000 to 3000 teeth during its lifetime so we won't complain about having to floss our measly 32.

Wasn't it smart of God to...

... make the large cumulonimbus cloud hold enough water for 500,000 baths. (That would take care of a lot of Saturday nights in my neck of the woods!)

... have the spider be the first website designer.

... give the humpback whale a call that is louder than a jetliner engine. (This vocal volume tends to be matched by people behind us who never stop talking when we're trying to sleep or work on airplane flights.)

Wasn't it smart of God to...

■■■ make the ostrich's eye bigger than its brain.
(This explains why, when they look at us
at the zoo, their expressions seem to say,
"I see your faces, but I don't think much of
them!")

■■■ lead the way in recycling by making coal
and other fossil fuels out of the vegetation
and creatures that were destroyed long ago
(perhaps during the flood in Noah's day).

Wasn't it smart of God to...

... make our arms and palms work like oars and our feet like flippers so we can hopefully swim faster than the big fish that like to eat our oars and flippers.

... design some snail species capable of sleeping for three years. (Perhaps the names of some of them are sophomores, juniors, and seniors!)

... make our skin develop calluses with regular use instead of shredding. (Otherwise there'd be no Bluegrass music to enjoy!)

... make it impossible for us to make gigantic things, such as skyscrapers, bridges, and machinery, without teamwork. (And just think how amazing it is that God alone stretched out the heavens!)

... give us daily sunrises and sunsets in multicolors that help us predict the coming weather. (This is a perfect tool for sailors, fishermen, farmers, shepherds, travelers, and people planning yard sales.)

... not allow wisdom to be purchasable. (Otherwise only the wealthiest of us would be wise.)

[Wisdom] cannot be bought with the finest gold, nor can its price be weighed in silver... "The fear of the Lord—that is wisdom, and to shun evil is understanding" [Job 28:15,28].

••• design light and objects to make shadows. (Otherwise there would be no sundials, no hand shades for the eyes, and no relief from the blazing sun under trees and behind large rocks. And we wouldn't understand these beautiful and comforting words: "Whoever dwells in the shelter of the Most High will rest in the shadow of the Almighty"—Psalm 91:1.)

••• give us chiggers so scratching feels so good.

... give us hips to use as baby rests.

... give us gnats to test our patience and tongue control.

... give instructions to parents to not spare the rod of discipline so the rest of us won't mind being around their kids.

Wasn't it smart of God to...

... design the wild turkey to show its emotions by color changes in its head and neck. (The colors range from light blue to deep red. Hue changes are especially useful for hunters: Pale blue means the bird is frightened; brilliant red means "Aim here!")

... give us sugar so we can smile when we eat rhubarb or lemon pie.

... gift some individuals with the skill of dentistry so they can fix the smiles of those who have enjoyed way too much rhubarb or lemon pie.

Wasn't it smart of God to...

... make dirt and then create man from it so that whether we're unlearned or intelligent, poor or wealthy, we all know where we got our start.

... design the human body to self-maintain by feeling thirsty when it needs water, hungry when it needs fuel, tired when it needs rest—and grumpy when any of those needs aren't met.

Wasn't it smart of God to...

••• give mice and other rodents an appetite for the calcium in shed antlers so they'll gnaw on them until they're gone, thus cleaning up nature's "litter."

••• allow so much to be said with a simple sigh. (Love, anger, resignation, frustration, exhaustion, exasperation, and relief are on the list, but none may be as sweet and satisfying as "It is finished!")

More Great Books by
Steve and Annie Chapman

More insights on Faith, Life, and Hunting by Steve Chapman

365 Things Every Hunter Should Know

If you love to hunt, you'll thoroughly enjoy the hunting secrets, insights, fascinating facts, and funny foibles in this book. Discover—

- how to survive between hunting seasons
- ways to encourage your mate to support your hunting habit
- tips for making your hunts more successful
- steps to make every hunt safer
- how to get your kids enthusiastic about hunting

Packed with entertaining and useful information, this handy pocket guide is perfect for taking on hunts and enjoying at home.

Great Hunting Stories

*Sunrise in the woods...birds singing...
turkeys calling, crunching leaves signaling
an approaching deer*

From a heart-pounding encounter with a bear to parting with a beloved rifle, these great hunting tales reveal the passion, excitement, skills, relationships, and yes, even spiritual growth, you—and every hunter—live for. Avid outdoorsman Steve Chapman reveals the heart and soul of hunting in these entertaining stories built around real-life adventures.

You'll find nuggets of truth and sage advice in gripping accounts that include how...

- time in a tree stand and knowledge of deer enhanced a marriage

- a dad's wisdom helped a young woman stand tall for hunting and faith

- tracking a wounded deer helped a father and son finally connect

Relive the enthusiasm and joy of the "fair chase" in these stories that will touch your heart, make your bow and trigger fingers twitch, and remind you of God's love and the wonderful world He created.

The Good Husband's Guide to Balancing Hobbies and Marriage

Steve Chapman candidly admits there have been times when his hobby has threatened his happy marriage. To win his wife's favor, Steve began a prayerful search for ways to help her appreciate his love for the outdoors. The process yielded 10 very practical ways to help you—

- balance your family finances and hobby gear
- spend meaningful time with your wife
- give her time alone by involving your kids in your interest
- address your wife's feelings or fears
- use the key of good communication

Whether your passion is hunting, golf, sports, gardening, or something else, this guide will help you keep your marriage happy while you do what you love to do.

Hot Topics for Couples

What are the hot-button issues every couple struggles with? Drawing on 30-plus years of marriage, biblical wisdom, and survey responses, Steve and Annie reveal the difficult areas and offer practical ways to navigate them. You'll discover straightforward advice and conversation starters on topics that include...

- gender differences in sexuality
- "honey dos" and "honey don'ts" for both spouses
- leading, following, and making it work
- money, money, money
- the ups and downs of change

As an added bonus, interactive questions will help you and your mate develop an even stronger relationship. You can build a dynamic marriage based on love, cooperation, and flexibility that will become more joyful and satisfying every year!

Steve and Annie Chapman's books
are available at your local Christian bookstore
or you can order them at

www.steveandanniechapman.com